PIANO • VOCAL • GUITAR

THE Frank Sinatra
ANTHOLOGY

Cover photo © Herman Leonard Photography, LLC
Photos bearing the PoPsie logo by William "PoPsie" Randolph
www.PoPsiePhotos.com
All other interior photos by Photofest

ISBN 1-4234-0485-8

HAL•LEONARD
CORPORATION
7777 W. BLUEMOUND RD. P.O. BOX 13819 MILWAUKEE, WI 5

Visit Hal Leonard Online at
www.halleonard.com

Contents

Frank Sinatra

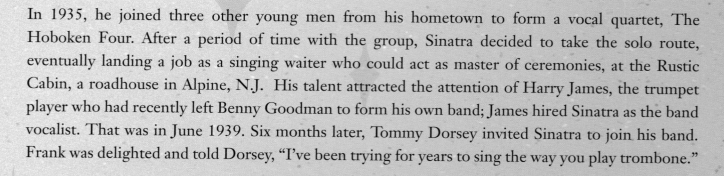

Francis Albert Sinatra—Ol' Blue Eyes, The Chairman of the Board, The Voice—was the greatest singer in American pop history and one of the most successful entertainers of the 20th century. His show business career spanned seven decades and included recordings, film and television, as well as innumerable performances in concert halls, sports stadiums, and nightclubs.

Born December 12, 1915 in Hoboken, New Jersey, Sinatra was the only child of Anthony Martin Sinatra, and his wife, Natalie Garavante, who was called Dolly. As a youngster, Frank dreamed of becoming an engineer and attending the Stevens Institute in Hoboken. That ambition didn't last long once he saw Bing Crosby perform in Jersey City in 1935. He would become a singer, he decided, and Dolly encouraged her son's aspiration.

In 1935, he joined three other young men from his hometown to form a vocal quartet, The Hoboken Four. After a period of time with the group, Sinatra decided to take the solo route, eventually landing a job as a singing waiter who could act as master of ceremonies, at the Rustic Cabin, a roadhouse in Alpine, N.J. His talent attracted the attention of Harry James, the trumpet player who had recently left Benny Goodman to form his own band; James hired Sinatra as the band vocalist. That was in June 1939. Six months later, Tommy Dorsey invited Sinatra to join his band. Frank was delighted and told Dorsey, "I've been trying for years to sing the way you play trombone."

With Dorsey's orchestra, the classic Sinatra crooning began and the idol started to form. Six months after joining the ensemble, he scored his first #1 hit, "I'll Never Smile Again," a dreamy ballad he sang with the Pied Pipers, the band's vocal group. Sinatra remained with Dorsey from January 1940 to September 1942. In December 1942, determined to be the first singer since Crosby to have a successful solo career, he appeared at the Paramount Theatre in New York City. Benny Goodman was the headliner on the program, with Sinatra billed as an "extra added attraction." When the bandleader introduced Mr. Sinatra, the audience erupted into a mass hysteria that made headlines. From 1943 to 1945, "The Voice" was the lead singer on radio's "Your Hit Parade." He also had his own show for several years, "Songs By Sinatra."

Sinatra's recorded legacy reveals a smooth, flexible baritone voice that he used with extraordinary skill. He recorded numerous hits for Columbia Records between 1943 and 1952, but moved to

Capitol Records in 1953. His collaborations with arrangers Nelson Riddle and Billy May produced some of the most popular albums of the time, including *Songs for Young Lovers*, *A Swingin' Affair*, *Come Fly with Me*, *Only the Lonely*, *In the Wee Small Hours*, and *Songs for Swingin' Lovers*. During this period, Sinatra went through a vocal evolution from crooning heartthrob to mature interpretive artist. Across the decades, the long-lined *legato* phrasing that made bobby-soxers swoon in the 1940s transformed popular singing, giving the lyrics a personal, intimate point of view. During the 1960s, Sinatra established his own recording company, Reprise Records, and released several hit albums, such as *Ring-a-Ding-Ding*, *September of My Years*, *My Way*, and *Strangers in the Night*. He also starred in a number of award-winning television specials.

A versatile actor as well as singer, Sinatra made his movie debut in 1941 and went on to appear in over 50 films. He won an Oscar for Best Supporting Actor for his portrayal of Maggio, the ill-fated G.I. in *From Here to Eternity* (1953). He also received a special Oscar for *The House I Live In* (1945), a 10-minute patriotic plea for racial and religious tolerance. During the course of his movie career, he played everything from a bashful sailor in *Anchors Aweigh* (1945) to a tormented drug addict in *The Man with the Golden Arm* (1955; Oscar nomination for Best Actor), a hard Army investigator in *The Manchurian Candidate* (1962) and a courageous prisoner of war in *Von Ryan's Express* (1965). His impressive filmography also includes *On the Town* (1945), *Guys and Dolls* (1955), *High Society* (1956), *Pal Joey* (1957), and *Ocean's Eleven* (1960).

In 1971, Sinatra announced his retirement from both recording and acting. He was far from finished, however; in 1973 he released the television special and album *Ol' Blue Eyes Is Back*. He appeared in the urban crime drama *The First Deadly Sin* in 1980, and made sporadic television and film appearances throughout the decade. The 1990s saw the release of two albums featuring Sinatra with other popular artists of his time, *Duets* (1993) and *Duets II* (1994). They outsold any of his previous recordings and proved that his style of music was still in demand.

Sinatra received numerous awards for his philanthropy and charitable deeds. In 1971, he was awarded the Jean Hersholt Humanitarian Award. He received the Kennedy Center Life Achievement Award in 1983 and the Presidential Medal of Freedom in 1985. The NAACP bestowed their Lifetime Achievement Award in 1987. Ten years later, he was granted the Congressional Gold Medal, the highest honor the United States can bestow upon a civilian.

Frank Sinatra has been called the most popular entertainer of the 20th century. Many would label him as one of the most generous philanthropists as well. During his lifetime, he donated more than one billion dollars to charities throughout the world.

Frank Sinatra passed away on May 14, 1998. In a career that spanned 60 years, Sinatra will remain a legend, living on through the body of work he left behind for generations to enjoy.

Ol' Blue Eyes

Sinatra Sings
Cole Porter

FRANK SINATRA IN PERSON!
THE Fabulous DORSEYS Tommy and Jimmy and Orch. JOEY BISHOP
ONE WEEK ONLY

SINATRA *Sings* **GERSHWIN**

What Sinatra did was important: he took the songs of Porter, Gershwin, Arlen, Cahn, Fain, and others and made them seem personal and imperative. It was an eloquent display of his paradoxical brand of artistry: tough yet sensitive, vain yet compassionate, grasping yet generous. And when Sinatra left the stage, we realized we might never witness artistry that big and that provocative again.

–*Rolling Stone*, 1980

The Croon Prince of Swing

Frank Sinatra

Orchestra conducted by Nelson Riddle

SWING EASY!

Capitol

The Pack Master

LIVE AND SWINGIN'

The Ultimate Rat Pack Collection

Frank Sinatra · Dean Martin · Sammy Davis, Jr. — Robin and the 7 Hoods

Co-Starring PETER FALK · Barbara Rush · Victor Buono and Bing Crosby as Allan A. Dale · A P-C PRODUCTION · TECHNICOLOR® · PANAVISION® · FROM WARNER BROS.

Whatever else has been said
about me personally is
unimportant. When I sing,
I believe, I'm honest.

–Frank Sinatra

ring-a-ding ding!

FRANK SINATRA   OCEAN'S 11
DEAN MARTIN
SAMMY DAVIS Jr.   PETER LAWFORD   ANGIE DICKINSON

Moonlight Sinatra

> You only live once, and the way I live, once is enough.
> —Frank Sinatra

MOONLIGHT SINATRA
arranged and conducted by NELSON RIDDLE

MOONLIGHT BECOMES YOU / MOON SONG / MOONLIGHT
SERENADE / REACHING FOR THE MOON /
I WISHED ON THE MOON / OH, YOU
CRAZY MOON / THE MOON GOT IN
MY EYES / MOONLIGHT MOOD /
MOON LOVE / THE MOON
WAS YELLOW
(And The Night
Was Young)

a Jolly Christmas from frank Sinatra

with the orchestra and chorus of GORDON JENKINS

The Voice

Come fly with me

FRANK SINATRA
with BILLY MAY and his orchestra

ni̇ce 'n' easy

Frank Sinatra
Songs for Young Lovers

VIOLETS FOR YOUR FURS
MY FUNNY VALENTINE • THE GIRL NEXT DOOR
A FOGGY DAY • LIKE SOMEONE IN LOVE
I GET A KICK OUT OF YOU • LITTLE GIRL BLUE
THEY CAN'T TAKE THAT AWAY FROM ME

Accompanied by NELSON RIDDLE

FRANK SINATRA

COME DANCE WITH ME!

with BILLY MAY and his orchestra

May you live to be 100, and may the last voice you hear be mine.

—Frank Sinatra

ALL OF ME

Words and Music by SEYMOUR SIMONS
and GERALD MARKS

ALL OR NOTHING AT ALL

Words by JACK LAWRENCE
Music by ARTHUR ALTMAN

Dm G7 G7♯5
might have been. No, I'd rath - er have noth - ing at
Cmaj9 C6 B♭m7 E♭7 A♭ A♭+
all. But, please, don't bring your
A♭6 A♭+ A♭ A♭maj7♯5 A♭6 A♭maj7♯5 E♭
lips so close to my cheek. Don't
A♭ A♭maj7♯5 D♭/A♭ A♭ E♭9 Cm/E♭
smile, or I'll be lost be - yond re - call.
3fr
4fr

AUTUMN IN NEW YORK

Words and Music by
VERNON DUKE

Slowly, poco rubato

It's time to end my lone-ly hol-i-day ____ and bid the coun-try a has-ty fare-well.

So on this gray and mel-an-chol-y day I'll move ____ to a Man-hat-tan ho-tel. I'll dis-

ALL THE WAY

Words by SAMMY CAHN
Music by JAMES VAN HEUSEN

APRIL IN PARIS

Words by E.Y. HARBURG
Music by VERNON DUKE

THE BEST IS YET TO COME

Words by CAROLYN LEIGH
Music by CY COLEMAN

THE BIRTH OF THE BLUES
from GEORGE WHITE'S SCANDALS OF 1926

Words by B.G. DeSYLVA and LEW BROWN
Music by RAY HENDERSON

48

CHICAGO
(That Toddlin' Town)

Words and Music by
FRED FISHER

Medium Bounce

Lyrics:
Chi - ca - go, ___ Chi - ca - go, ___ that tod - dl - in' town, ___ (tod - dl - in' town,) Chi - ca - go, ___ Chi - ca - go, ___ I'll show you a - round. ___ I love it!

CALL ME IRRESPONSIBLE

from the Paramount Picture PAPA'S DELICATE CONDITION

Words by SAMMY CAHN
Music by JAMES VAN HEUSEN

COME DANCE WITH ME

Words by SAMMY CAHN
Music by JAMES VAN HEUSEN

COME RAIN OR COME SHINE

from ST. LOUIS WOMAN

Words by JOHNNY MERCER
Music by HAROLD ARLEN

Slow Blues feel

I'm gon-na love you like no-bod-y's loved you, come rain or come shine. _____

High as a moun-tain and deep as a riv-er, come

rain or come shine. _____ I guess when you

COME FLY WITH ME

Words by SAMMY CAHN
Music by JAMES VAN HEUSEN

they'd blush and speak of hon-ey-moon-ing. And if your mem-o-ry re-

calls, they spoke of Ni-ag-'ra Falls. _____ But to-

day, my dar-ling, to-day, when you meet the one you love, you

Moderately, with a strong beat

say: _____ Come fly with me! ___ Let's fly! ___

CYCLES

Words and Music by
GAYLE CALDWELL

Moderately

So I'm down, and and so I'm
I've been told, and and I be -
But I'll keep my head up

out, that life but so are man - y oth - ers.
lieve that life is meant for liv - in'.
high, al - though I'm kind - a tired. _____

72

DANCING ON THE CEILING

Words by LORENZ HART
Music by RICHARD RODGERS

DAY IN—DAY OUT

Words by JOHNNY MERCER
Music by RUBE BLOOM

DON'T TAKE YOUR LOVE FROM ME

Words and Music by
HENRY NEMO

DON'T WORRY 'BOUT ME
from COTTON CLUB PARADE

Lyric by TED KOEHLER
Music by RUBE BLOOM

Lyrics:

This is the one mo-ment that I thought I nev-er could live through, but

now some-how, that it's here, my dear, that fool-ish fear dis-ap-pears, and

say - ing good - bye seems sweet. _____ It's plain that

EASY TO LOVE
(You'd Be So Easy to Love)
from BORN TO DANCE

Words and Music by
COLE PORTER

Lyrics:
You'd be so eas-y to love, so eas-y to i-dol-ize, all oth-ers a-bove, so

FIVE MINUTES MORE

Lyric by SAMMY CAHN
Music by JULE STYNE

EMBRACEABLE YOU

from CRAZY FOR YOU

Music and Lyrics by GEORGE GERSHWIN
and IRA GERSHWIN

Lyrics:
Doz-ens of girls would storm up; I had to lock my door. Some-how I could-n't warm up to one be-fore. What was it that con-trolled me?

FLY ME TO THE MOON
(In Other Words)
featured in the Motion Picture ONCE AROUND

Words and Music by
BART HOWARD

FROM HERE TO ETERNITY

Words by ROBERT WELLS
Music by FRED KARGER

A FOGGY DAY

from A DAMSEL IN DISTRESS

Music and Lyrics by GEORGE GERSHWIN
and IRA GERSHWIN

THE GOOD LIFE

Words by JACK REARDON and JEAN BROUSSOLLE
Music by SACHA DISTEL

GOODY GOODY

Words and Music by JOHNNY MERCER
and MATT MALNECK

HEY! JEALOUS LOVER

Words and Music by SAMMY CAHN,
KAY TWOMEY and BEE WALKER

With a solid beat

HIGH HOPES

Words by SAMMY CAHN
Music by JAMES VAN HEUSEN

HOW DEEP IS THE OCEAN
(How High Is the Sky)

Words and Music by
IRVING BERLIN

HOW LITTLE WE KNOW

Words by CAROLYN LEIGH
Music by PHILIP SPRINGER

Rhythmically, but not fast

How lit - tle we know _____ how much to dis - cov - er _____ what chem - i - cal forc - es flow _____ from lov - er to lov - er? _____ How lit - tle we

I CAN'T GET STARTED WITH YOU

from ZIEGFELD FOLLIES

Words by IRA GERSHWIN
Music by VERNON DUKE

I FALL IN LOVE TOO EASILY

Words by SAMMY CAHN
Music by JULE STYNE

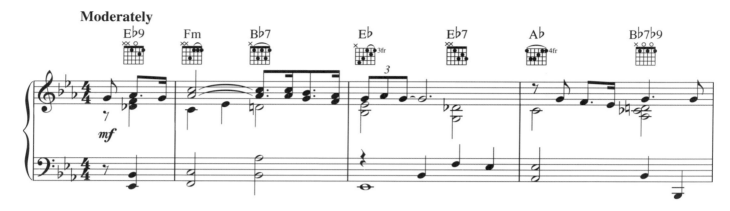

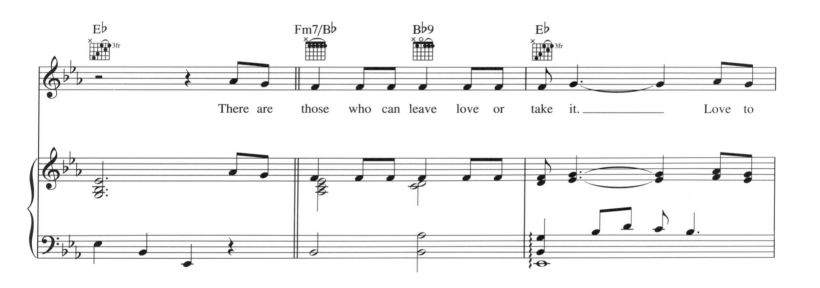

There are those who can leave love or take it. _____ Love to
them is just what they make it. _____ I wish that I were the

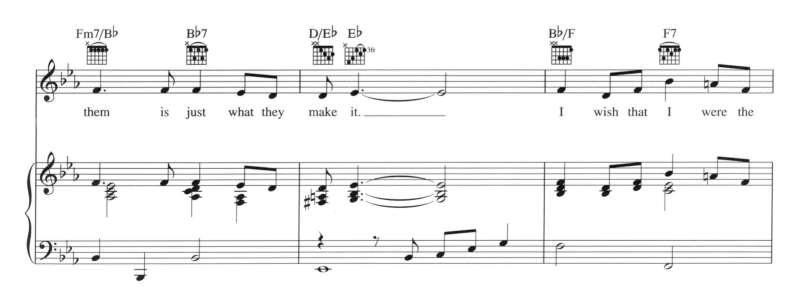

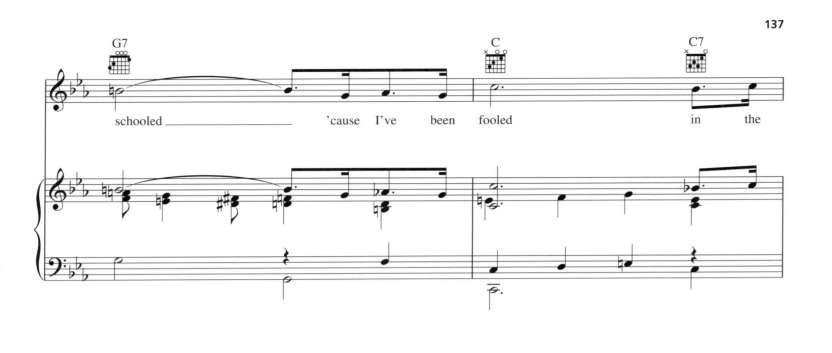

schooled _____ 'cause I've been fooled in the

past. _____ And still I fall _____ in love too eas-i-ly, ___

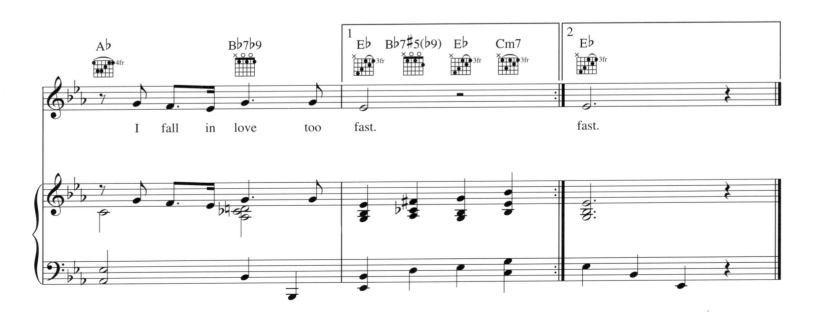

I fall in love too fast. fast.

I GET A KICK OUT OF YOU

from ANYTHING GOES

Words and Music by
COLE PORTER

I GUESS I'LL HANG MY TEARS OUT TO DRY

from GLAD TO SEE YOU

Words by SAMMY CAHN
Music by JULE STYNE

Slowly

The torch I car-ry is hand-some; _____ it's worth its heart-ache in ran-som. _____ And when the twi-light steals, I know how the la-dy in the har-bor feels. _____ When I want rain, _____

I HADN'T ANYONE TILL YOU

Words and Music by
RAY NOBLE

Slowly, with expression

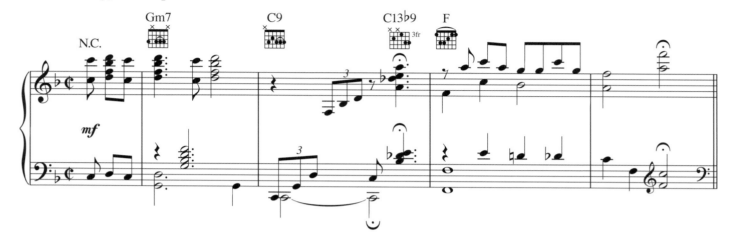

I'll ad-mit an oc-ca-sion-al af-fair, __ but some-how they all made me

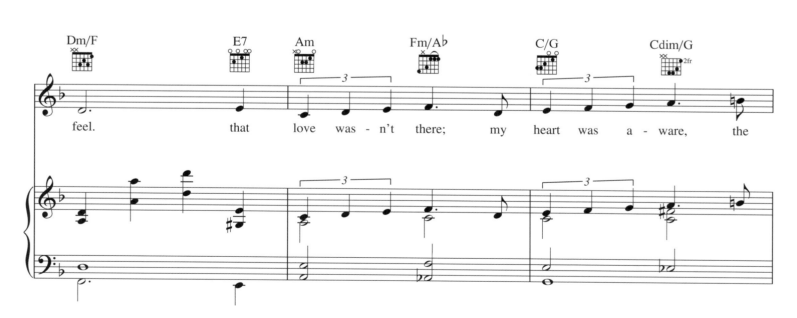

feel. that love was-n't there; my heart was a-ware, the

B♭/D
B♭m/D♭
C7
Dm
lie a - wake and won - der if there could be a
A/E
B9
E7
A7
Adim
some - one in the wide world just made for me.
rit.
Gm7
C7
Gm7
C9
Now I see, I had to save my love for
a tempo
F
Am7
D9
4fr
D7
you, I nev - er gave my love till

I THOUGHT ABOUT YOU

Words by JOHNNY MERCER
Music by JIMMY VAN HEUSEN

Seems that I read, _ or some-bod-y said _ that out of sight is out of mind. _ May-be that's so ___ but I tried to go _____ and leave you be-hind. ___

I WANNA BE AROUND

Words and Music by JOHNNY MERCER
and SADIE VIMMERSTEDT

I'LL BE AROUND

Words and Music by
ALEC WILDER

Your lat-est love can nev-er last, and when it's past, I'll be a-round when {he's}{she's} gone. _____ Good-bye a-gain, and

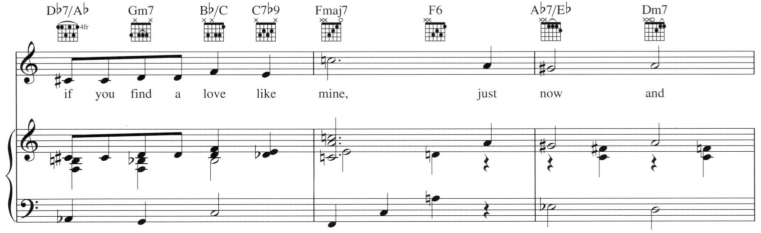

if you find a love like mine, just now and

I'LL BE SEEING YOU

Lyric by IRVING KAHAL
Music by SAMMY FAIN

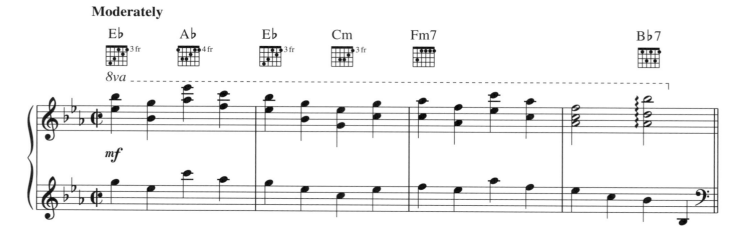

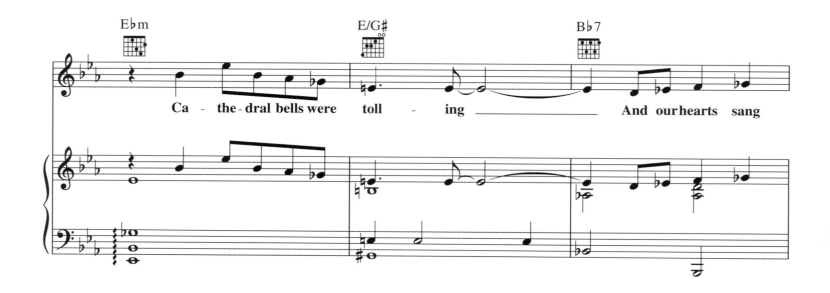

Ca - the-dral bells were toll - ing _____ And our hearts sang

on, _____ Was it the spell of Par - is _____

I'LL NEVER SMILE AGAIN

Words and Music by
RUTH LOWE

I'M A FOOL TO WANT YOU

Words and Music by JACK WOLF,
JOEL HERRON and FRANK SINATRA

Moderately, with expression

I'm a fool to want you, ___

I'm a fool to want you, ___ to want a

love that can't be true, a love that's there for oth-ers, too. ___

I'VE GOT A CRUSH ON YOU

Music and Lyrics by GEORGE GERSHWIN
and IRA GERSHWIN

Lightly, playfully

He: How
She: How

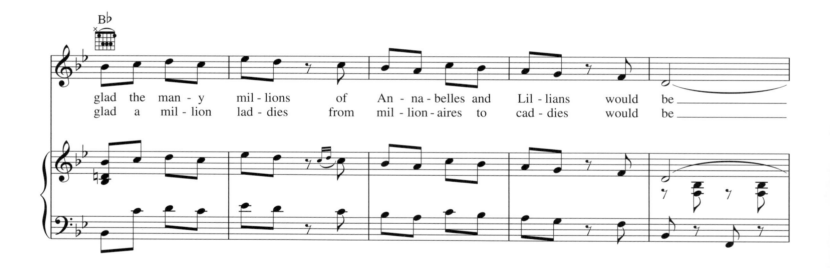

glad the man-y mil-lions of An-na-belles and Lil-lians would be ___
glad a mil-lion lad-dies from mil-lion-aires to cad-dies would be ___

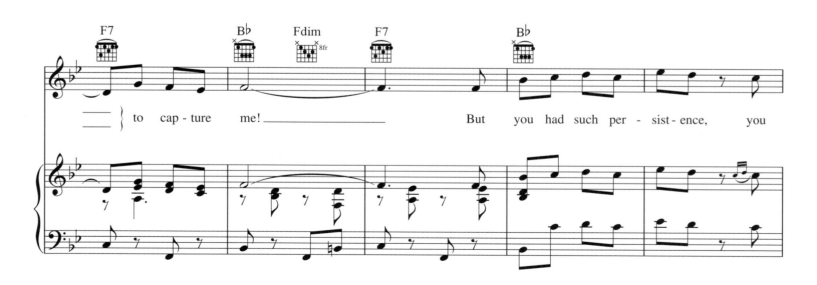

___ to cap-ture me! ___ But you had such per-sist-ence, you

I'VE GOT THE WORLD ON A STRING

Lyric by TED KOEHLER
Music by HAROLD ARLEN

I'VE GOT YOU UNDER MY SKIN
from BORN TO DANCE

Words and Music by
COLE PORTER

IN THE BLUE OF EVENING

Words by TOM ADAIR
Music by D'ARTEGA

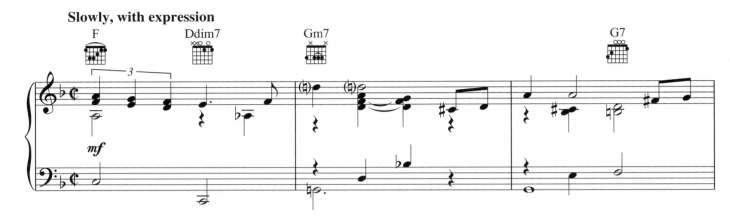

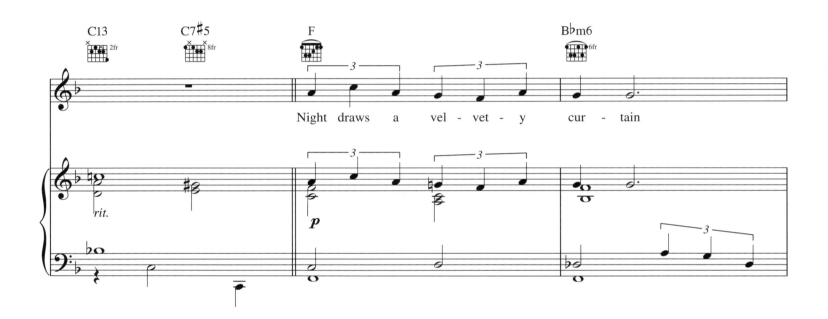

Night draws a vel-vet-y cur-tain

o-ver the cares of the day. My heart is light, for it's cer-tain that

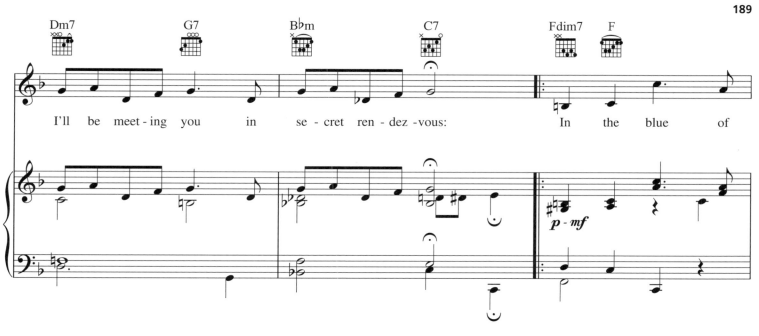

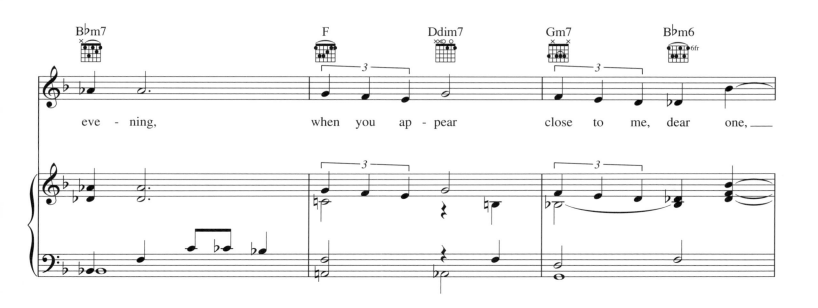

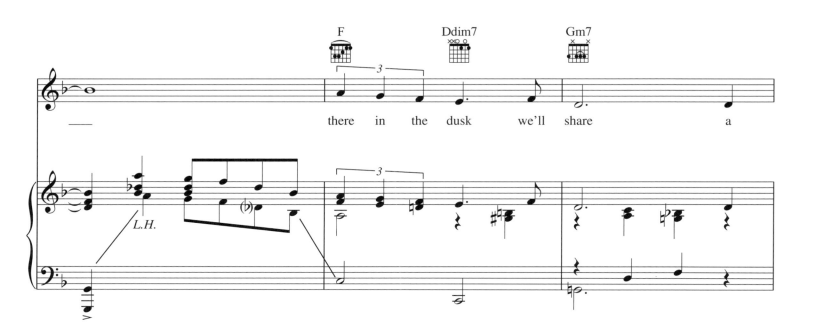

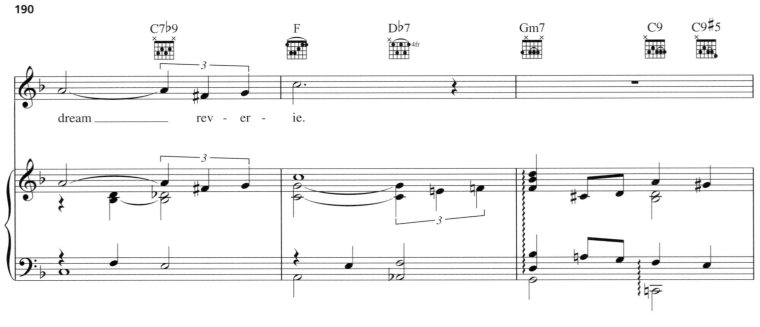

dream _____ rev - er - ie.

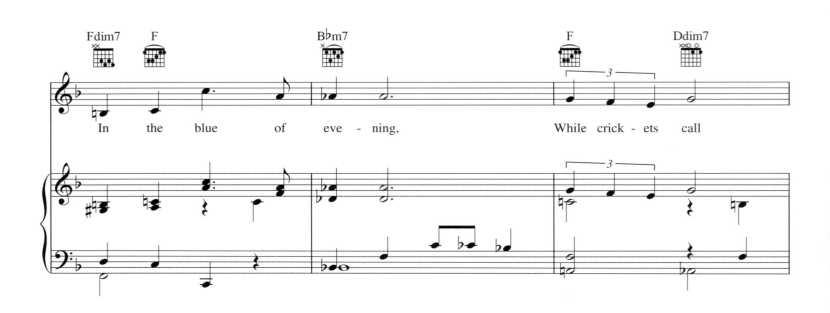

In the blue of eve - ning, While crick - ets call

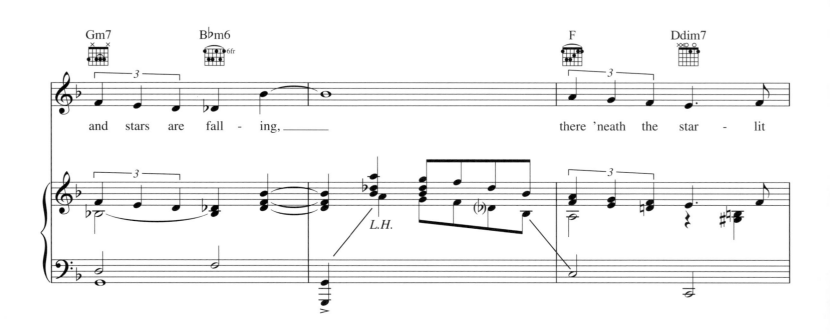

and stars are fall - ing, _____ there 'neath the star - lit

IN THE STILL OF THE NIGHT

Words and Music by
COLE PORTER

In the still of the night, as I gaze from my win - dow at the moon in its flight, my thoughts all

IN THE WEE SMALL HOURS OF THE MORNING

Words by BOB HILLIARD
Music by DAVID MANN

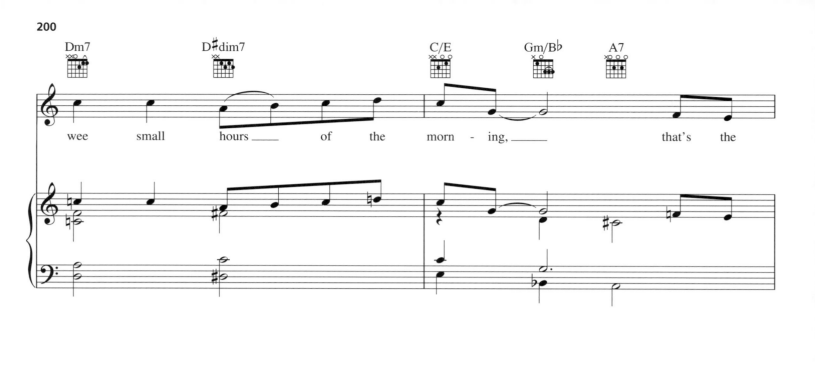

wee small hours ____ of the morn - ing, ____ that's the

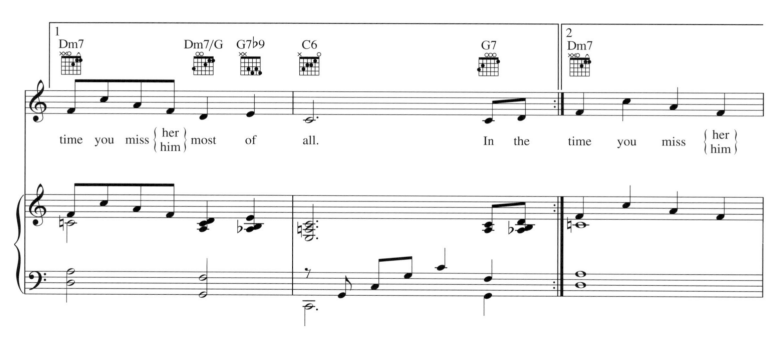

time you miss {her}{him} most of all. In the time you miss {her}{him}

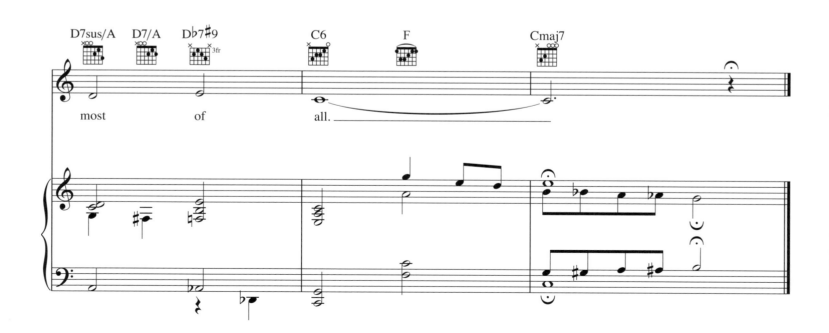

most of all. ____

IT ALL DEPENDS ON YOU

Words and Music by B.G. DeSYLVA,
LEW BROWN and RAY HENDERSON

IT HAPPENED IN MONTEREY

Words by BILLY ROSE
Music by MABEL WAYNE

JUST IN TIME

Words by BETTY COMDEN and ADOLPH GREEN
Music by JULE STYNE

209

IT NEVER ENTERED MY MIND

Words by LORENZ HART
Music by RICHARD RODGERS

Moderately

I don't care if there's pow-der on my nose, I don't care if my

hair-do is in place, I've lost the ver-y mean-ing of re-pose, I

nev-er put a mud pack on my face. Oh, who'd have thought that I'd

IT WAS A VERY GOOD YEAR

Words and Music by
ERVIN DRAKE

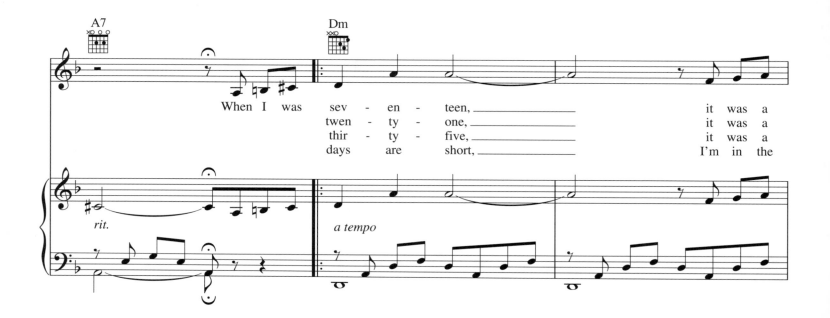

When I was sev - en - teen, _____ it was a
twen - ty - one, _____ it was a
thir - ty - five, _____ it was a
days are short, _____ I'm in the

ver - y good year, _____ it was a ver - y good year for
ver - y good year, _____ it was a ver - y good year for
ver - y good year, _____ it was a ver - y good year for
au - tumn of the year; _____ and now I think of my life as

JUST ONE OF THOSE THINGS

from HIGH SOCIETY

Words and Music by
COLE PORTER

THE LADY IS A TRAMP

Words by LORENZ HART
Music by RICHARD RODGERS

LEARNIN' THE BLUES

Words and Music by
DOLORES "VICKI" SILVERS

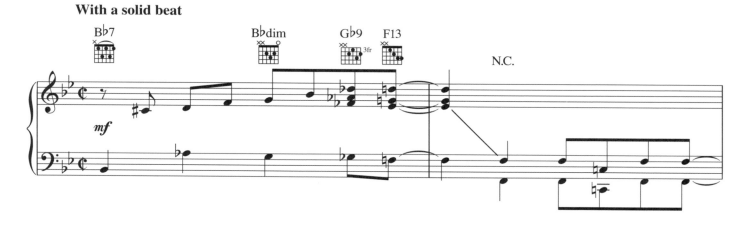

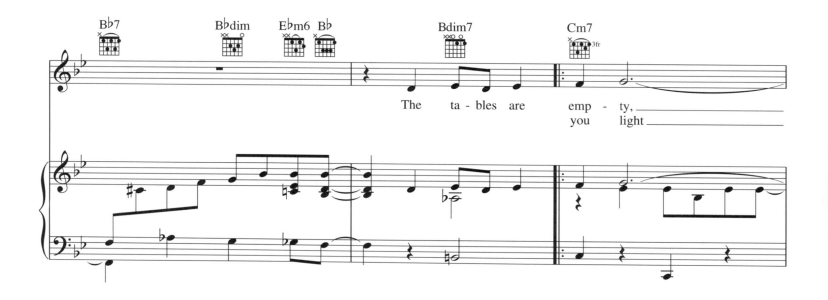

LET'S GET AWAY FROM IT ALL

Words and Music by TOM ADAIR
and MATT DENNIS

LOVE AND MARRIAGE

Words by SAMMY CAHN
Music by JAMES VAN HEUSEN

LIKE SOMEONE IN LOVE

Words by JOHNNY BURKE
Music by JIMMY VAN HEUSEN

LOVE'S BEEN GOOD TO ME

Words and Music by
ROD McKUEN

LUCK BE A LADY

By FRANK LOESSER

MY FUNNY VALENTINE

Words by LORENZ HART
Music by RICHARD RODGERS

made, thy va - cant brow and thy tous - led hair con -

ceal thy good in - tent. Thou no - ble, up - right,

truth - ful, sin - cere and slight - ly dop - ey gent, you're

my }
My } fun - ny val - en - tine, sweet com - ic

MY HEART STOOD STILL

Words by LORENZ HART
Music by RICHARD RODGERS

MY KIND OF TOWN
(Chicago Is)

Words by SAMMY CAHN
Music by JAMES VAN HEUSEN

MY WAY

English Words by PAUL ANKA
Original French Words by GILLES THIBAULT
Music by JACQUES REVAUX and CLAUDE FRANCOIS

266

NANCY
(With the Laughing Face)

Words by PHIL SILVERS
Music by JAMES VAN HEUSEN

NICE 'N' EASY

Words and Music by LEW SPENCE,
ALAN BERGMAN and MARILYN BERGMAN

THEME FROM "NEW YORK, NEW YORK"

Words by FRED EBB
Music by JOHN KANDER

NICE WORK IF YOU CAN GET IT

Music and Lyrics by GEORGE GERSHWIN
and IRA GERSHWIN

OH! LOOK AT ME NOW

Words by JOHN DeVRIES
Music by JOE BUSHKIN

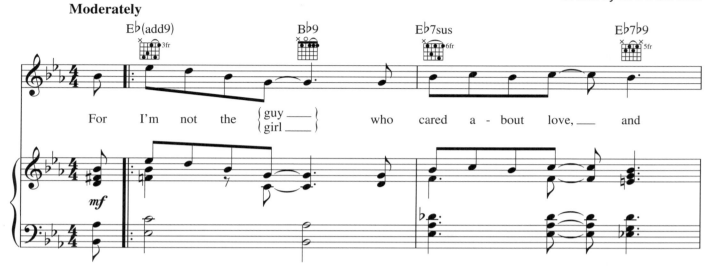

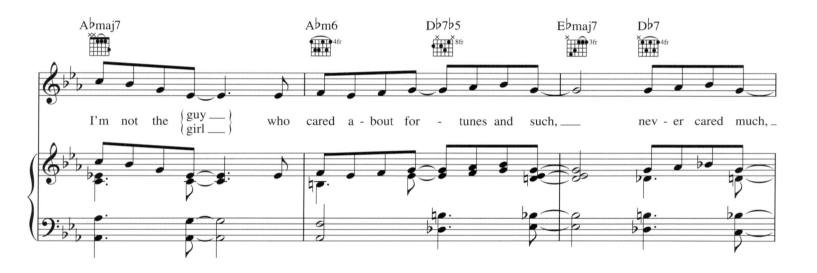

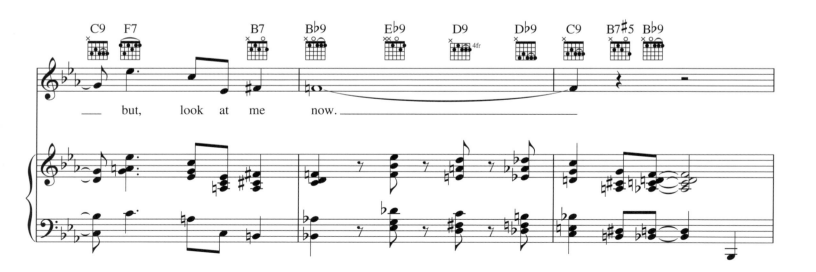

NIGHT AND DAY

from GAY DIVORCE

Words and Music by
COLE PORTER

ONE FOR MY BABY
(And One More for the Road)
from the Motion Picture THE SKY'S THE LIMIT

Lyric by JOHNNY MERCER
Music by HAROLD ARLEN

POCKETFUL OF MIRACLES

Words by SAMMY CAHN
Music by JAMES VAN HEUSEN

PUT YOUR DREAMS AWAY
(For Another Day)

Lyric by RUTH LOWE
Music by STEPHAN WEISS and PAUL MANN

SAME OLD SATURDAY NIGHT

Words by SAMMY CAHN
Music by FRANK REARDON

Moderate beat

Went to see a mov-ie show, ___
Then I made the u-sual stop, ___

found my-self an emp-ty row. ___   Thought the show was
cof-fee at the cof-fee shop. ___   Friend-ly face no-

RIVER, STAY 'WAY FROM MY DOOR

Lyric by MORT DIXON
Music by HARRY WOODS

SATURDAY NIGHT
(Is the Loneliest Night of the Week)

Words by SAMMY CAHN
Music by JULE STYNE

THE SECOND TIME AROUND

Lyric by SAMMY CAHN
Music by JAMES VAN HEUSEN

SOMEONE TO WATCH OVER ME

Music and Lyrics by GEORGE GERSHWIN
and IRA GERSHWIN

THE SEPTEMBER OF MY YEARS

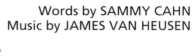

Words by SAMMY CAHN
Music by JAMES VAN HEUSEN

SEPTEMBER SONG

Words by MAXWELL ANDERSON
Music by KURT WEILL

THE SONG IS YOU

Lyrics by OSCAR HAMMERSTEIN II
Music by JEROME KERN

let you know the song my heart would sing, _____ that beau - ti - ful

rhap - so - dy of love and youth and spring? _____ The mu - sic is

sweet, _____ the words are true, _____ the song is

you. _____

STRANGERS IN THE NIGHT
adapted from A MAN COULD GET KILLED

Words by CHARLES SINGLETON
and EDDIE SNYDER
Music by BERT KAEMPFERT

TALK TO ME

Words and Music by EDDIE SNYDER,
RUDY VALEE and STAN KAHAN

SUMMER WIND

English Words by JOHNNY MERCER
Original German Lyrics by HANS BRADTKE
Music by HENRY MAYER

(Love Is)
THE TENDER TRAP

Words by SAMMY CAHN
Music by JAMES VAN HEUSEN

THAT'S LIFE

Words and Music by DEAN KAY
and KELLY GORDON

That's life, that's what peo - ple say.

You're rid - in' high in A - pril, shot down in May; but I

know I'm gon - na change that tune when I'm

THERE'S NO YOU

Words and Music by TOM ADAIR
and HAL HOPPER

THEY ALL LAUGHED

Music and Lyrics by GEORGE GERSHWIN
and IRA GERSHWIN

They all laughed at Chris-to-pher Co-lum-bus when he said the world was round.
They all laughed at Rock-e-fel-ler Cen-ter, now they're fight-ing to get in.

They all laughed when Ed-i-son re-cord-ed sound.
They all laughed at Whit-ney and his cot-ton gin.

They all laughed at
They all laughed at

THEY CAN'T TAKE THAT AWAY FROM ME

Music and Lyrics by GEORGE GERSHWIN
and IRA GERSHWIN

Fm7 B♭7sus B♭7 Fm7 A♭/B♭ E♭ B♭7♯5
the mem-'ry of all that,
E♭9 A♭7♭5 Gm7♭5 A♭ Fm7 C9 F7 A♭/B♭
no, no, they can't take that a-way from me! The way your smile just beams,
E♭ Fm7/B♭ E♭/G G♭dim Fm7 B♭7sus B♭7
the way you sing off key,
Fm7 A♭/B♭ E♭ B♭7♯5 E♭9 A♭7♭5 Gm7♭5
the way you haunt my dreams, no, no, they

THREE COINS IN THE FOUNTAIN

from THREE COINS IN THE FOUNTAIN

Words by SAMMY CAHN
Music by JULE STYNE

TIME AFTER TIME

Words by SAMMY CAHN
Music by JULE STYNE

TOO MARVELOUS FOR WORDS

Words by JOHNNY MERCER
Music by RICHARD A. WHITING

THE VERY THOUGHT OF YOU

Words and Music by
RAY NOBLE

THE WAY YOU LOOK TONIGHT

Words by DOROTHY FIELDS
Music by JEROME KERN

WHAT IS THIS THING CALLED LOVE?

Words and Music by
COLE PORTER

WITCHCRAFT

Lyric by CAROLYN LEIGH
Music by CY COLEMAN

YOU MAKE ME FEEL SO YOUNG

Words by MACK GORDON
Music by JOSEF MYROW

Do I _____ seem as cheer-ful as a school-boy play-ing hook-ey? _____ Do I _____ seem to gur-gle like a ba-by with a cook-ie? _____

run - ning a - cross a mead - ow, ___ pick - ing up lots ___ of for -

get - me - nots. ___ You make me feel so young, ___

you make me feel there are songs to be sung, bells to be rung, and a

won - der - ful fling to be flung. And e - ven when I'm old and

YOU BROUGHT A NEW KIND OF LOVE TO ME

from the Paramount Picture THE BIG POND

Words and Music by SAMMY FAIN,
IRVING KAHAL and PIERRE NORMAN

YOU GO TO MY HEAD

Words by HAVEN GILLESPIE
Music by J. FRED COOTS

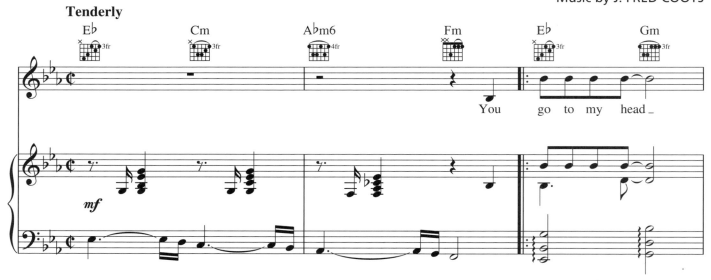

You go to my head _

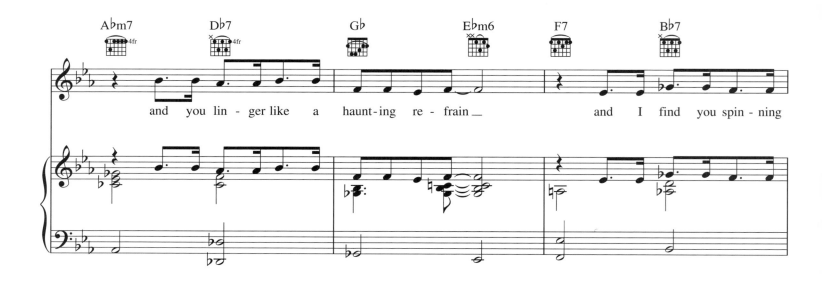

and you lin - ger like a haunt-ing re - frain _ and I find you spin - ning

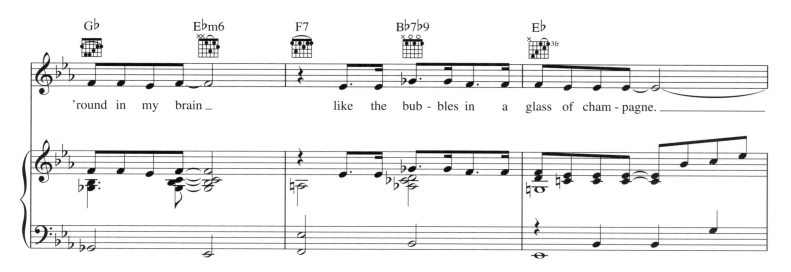

'round in my brain _ like the bub - bles in a glass of cham - pagne. _

YOU'D BE SO NICE TO COME HOME TO

Words and Music by
COLE PORTER

YOUNG AT HEART

Words by CAROLYN LEIGH
Music by JOHNNY RICHARDS